DATE DUE

HANDBOOK OF FLORIDA

Palms

By BETH McGEACHY

Designed by

Great Outdoors Association

Ruba Allyn

PRESIDENT

★　★　★

THIRD EDITION

★　★　★

Manufactured in the United States of America
The Great Outdoors Publishing Co.
4747 - 28th Street North, St. Petersburg, Florida 33714

Standard Book No. 8200 - 0404 - 9

ACKNOWLEDGEMENTS

We hope that with actual photographs as well as drawings for your guide, you will learn to identify the more common varieties and be able to call them by name. Unable of course to include all palms, we have tried to select those most often seen in outdoor Florida.

It is impossible to acknowledge appropriately the helpful assistance of the many who offered encouragement and interest, of those who helped in the assembling and clarifying of the material, of those who helped in the identification. To all, thanks are due. I should be remiss, however, if I did not mention by name: Miss Sarah Byers, Clearwater Public Library; Arnett Brown of the Seminole Nurseries; A. W. Downing of Pinellas Nursery; J. S. Pecarek of the Largo Sentinel; Dr. John Davis of the University of Florida and Lucita Hardie Wait of Miami. They were generous with their knowledge and their time.

Special thanks is tendered to Fred Walden, author of A Dictionary or Trees, for the use of his drawings and his text for research in the palm-like plants. Rube Allyn furnished the beautiful cover photograph of a Royal Palm.

Without these helpful friends, this book might never have been completed.

B. McG.

3

SOURCE MATERIAL

Bulletin 152 *Native and Exotic Palms of Florida* by Harold Mowry. Published by Agricultural Extension service of the University of Florida, Gainesville, Florida (A revision of Bulletin 84).

Bulletin 261 *Ornamental Trees* by Harold Mowry. Published as above.

Bulletin 22 *Palm Trees in the United States*. Agricultural information from the Department of Agriculture, Washington, D. C.

Botanical Papers from Fairchild Tropical Garden *The Major Kinds of Palms* by Alex Hawkes.

Photography by: The Bergeson's .... Clearwater
Gatteri .... Miami, Fla.
Bob Moore .... Clearwater
George Fulmer .... Clearwater

About the Author

Beth McGeachy is a North Carolinian. She was born in Wilmington, living there in her youth and going back later to teach, after her graduation from Agnes Scott College. She has lived in the South with her minister husband, Dr. D. P. McGeachy, Jr., and for the last 18 years they have been in Florida where Dr. McGeachy has served as minister at Peace Memorial Presbyterian Church, Clearwater.

Besides her family, which consists of her husband and three children, Mrs. McGeachy's main interest has been her church, with especial emphasis on the Christian education of children.

All of her life she had been interested in the world around her and has, she says, an insatiable curiosity about what lives and grows in it. She likes to know the plants and animals around her so that she can call them by name.

Mrs. McGeachy said that when she moved to Florida she was particularly fascinated by the Palms. Few persons could tell her their names—and those few were seldom available. She did what anyone else could have done. She searched for information; read all available material—and asked questions.

Her particular interest was in the Palms growing out of doors. The ones everyone could see. As she began to learn about them, she wanted others to know. She started collecting pictures and information—and this book was born. From it she hopes that many others will be interested to do what she did: Look, read and ask questions.

BETH McGEACHY

5

Foreword

FLORIDA is a land of Palms and consequently a land of beauty. From the Pigmy Date with its finely cut leaves to the tall Washingtonia that tosses its fronds in the wind, looking forsooth, like an Indian chief in his war bonnet; from the creeping Saw Palmetto to the mighty Royal, the Palms are symbols of the exotic lands from whence they come.

A Palm is not just a Palm. Each of the estimated 3,000 species has its own individuality. Several hundred of these Palms have come from various tropical countries of the world to join the native Palms of Florida, each making a special contribution, both in beauty and usefulness.

In making a study of Palms, we find they are divided into two groups, according to their leaf characteristics. One of these classes is "pinnate" or feather-leafed, the other is "Palmate" or fan-leafed, (see cut on another page.) By far the largest number of species are pinnate.

Palms are woody plants of varied habit. They range in size from those that grow a hundred feet or more to the ones that are only two feet high. Some grow as solitary trees, while some have clusters of tall trunks. Still others are bushy or scrubby.

The first leaves of all Palm seedlings look more or less alike and could easily be mistaken for grasses. The succeeding leaves begin to show the characteristic feather-like or fan-like shape. In some cases, however, a mature tree is needed for accurate identification.

Palm flowers are small and lily-like in plan, but are quite varied. They are most often very numerous and are grown within one or more protective, membraneous or woody structures that split or rupture to release them. The flowers of many plants are not complete for setting fruits, are either male or female. These two sexes are borne on the same or separate flower stalks, on the same tree or on separate trees.

Fruits, too, differ. The largest known is the double coconut (Lodoicea) weighing 40 pounds or more. The smallest is about the size of a pea (Euterpe). They are all somewhat like a peach or cherry in structure, with a kernel surrounded by a pulp that in turn varies in character and size.

MOST COMMON VARIETIES OF PALMS AND PALM-LIKE PLANTS

with directions and suggestions as to their care

The above picture shows two kinds of Palm leaves. On the left is the "pinnate" or feather-leafed. On the right the "palmate" or fan-leaf.

Palm Bloom

In this picture we see a closeup of a Palm bloom. and the Spadix in which it has been held.

Note the other spathes behind the open ones. These are almost mature. All Palms bloom in this manner. The fruit is set as the flowers drop off. This bloom from the Cocos plumosa is one of the handsomest.

SAW CABBAGE

Paurotis wrightii

The Saw Cabbage belongs in the cluster-forming species. From these clumps rise slender trees that at times reach the height of 40 feet. Their trunks are usually covered with red-brown leaf bases. They have as their foliage small, stiff, fan-shaped leaves. These leaves are divided about half way into numerous segments which are in turn deeply split.

In some localities this Palm is called Madeira. It is at home in southern Florida, Bahamas and Cuba.

The flowers are abundant but tiny blossoms. The fruit is reddish, globular, one-half inch in diameter.

CABBAGE PALM

Sabal palmetto

Also called Carolina Palm and Swamp Cabbage. Native to southeastern United States and Bahamas, ranges from North Carolina to Florida. In natural state generally found growing in large groups, close together, trunks encased in the plaited-like "bootjacks" of old leaf bases on the younger Palms. An occasional older specimen will have shed the "boots" and have a smooth trunk towering 40 to 60 feet.

Leaves fan-shaped, medium glossy green above, grayish-green underside, to seven feet long, alternate, deeply divided in drooping segments with thread-like fibers, on four to six foot stalks.

Flowers greenish-white, fragrant, one-fourth inch wide, in immense drooping clusters. Seed fruit one-half inch wide, round, blackish-brown.

The Cabbage Palm derives its common name from the fact that the leaf bud or "heart" at the top of the trunk is an edible delicacy with a fine cabbage flavor when cooked in the same manner as the vegetable. It was one of the chief foods of the early Florida Indians and today can be found in many stores,

The Cabbage Palm is the State Tree of Florida.

Group Planting of Palmettos

This picture shows a group planting of Palmettos in a yard in Clearwater, Florida. Note the "boots" on two of the trunks. These are the remains of old leaf stalks.

These Palms are also found growing in marshes, hammocks and sandy soil. They are at home in almost every part of Florida.

SAW PALMETTO   *Serenoa repens*

This is a very common Palm which grows throughout
the southern United States. It often covers huge areas
with a solid mass of creeping stems that have heads of
handsome leaves. These stems or trunks are usually
horizontal but at times grow into an erect plant of 10
feet. The fan-shaped leaves are nearly circular and
deeply cut into many divisions. The leaf color is generally green to yellowish green, but in some areas, main-
ly along the coast, many of the plants have a shiny bluish cast that is in striking contrast to the plants farther
north or inland. The leaf stalks are slender and are
armed with numerous small but very sharp spines.

This Saw Palmetto may be seen growing wild in almost any uncultivated area. It is often left to make
attractive clumps as land is developed.

The Saw Palmetto is closely allied to the genus
Sabal, but is a species in its own right. Its fan-like
leaves are most attractive but the plant itself is such
a prolific grower that it causes trouble when land is to
be cleared. The root system is difficult to remove.

The flowers are white, the fruit is blue-black and
oblong in shape, about one inch long. They are at home
in Florida and all of the southern states east of the Mis-
sissippi as far north as the Carolinas.

WASHINGTONIA PALM
Washingtonia robusta

Native to mexico and Lower California, this genus of American Fan Palms is grown extensively in California, Florida and gulf states.

W. robusta, species most commonly grown in Florida, is distinguished by its heavy growth, 80 to 100 feet, when mature and untrimmed and usually covered with shaggy mass of dead leaves, like a huge skirt, giving its nickname "Petticoat Palm."

The broad leaves resemble huge fans, measuring three to five feet across, accordian-pleated with up to 70 folds, borne on two and one-half to three feet spiny-edged, orange-brown stalks, first erect, then spreading and finally drooping.

Branched clusters of tiny white flowers are followed by round, lampblack seed fruits.

Highly salt resisting, flourishes in Florida near the bays and gulf from Jacksonville to Miami.

W. filifera is similar to W. robusta but better suited for drier inland climate of California, differing from the Robusta by having grey-green foliage and tough thread-like filaments around the outer edge.

The Washingtonias are the most widespread and popular of all the Palm groups in cultivation in sub-tropical countries.

13

Washingtonia

This picture was taken by the roadside. It shows a
Washingtonia that has not been trimmed.. When untrimmed the fronds will stay on for years. It is easy to
see how the Palm gets its nickname "Petticoat Palm."

Washingtonia

These Washingtonias are on the Memorial Cause-
way between Clearwater, Florida, and Clearwater
Beach. The picture shows the Phoenix canariensis between the tall Washingtonias. The inset is of a small
Washingtonia showing the characteristic stiff leaf.

Many Florida cities have streets lined with this
beautiful Palm.

COCOS PLUMOSA
Arecastrum romanzoffianum

Also called Feather Palm and Queen Palm.

Native to Brazil. Height, 40 to 60 feet, slender, grayish trunk 12 to 14 inches in diameter, larger at base, with rings of scar tissue of former leaf growth, shaggy, spreading crown.

Feathery leaves, or fronds, 10 to 15 feet long, gently arched, the fringe-like leaflets 10 to 12 inches long and one inch wide drooping from the two-to-three-inch-wide midrib.

Hard, woody bloom bracts four to six feet long, ribbed from tip to base, are borne in lower leaf sheaths and resemble a small canoe when the golden-yellow flower cluster is released. Orange-colored fruits one inch thick are borne along the 12-inch flower spikes growing laterally from the cane-like stem of the four-to-six-foot-long flower cluster. The hard-shelled fruit, or nut, when ripe and peeled from its thin fibrous husk has the familiar monkey-face of the coconut. Poisonous when green.

Propagation is by seed only which requires six months for germination. The round, nut-like seeds should be planted in moist, loamy soil about one or two inches deep.

Cocos Plumosa

    For its beauty and fairly rapid growth, this Palm is widely planted in Florida.

    The Cocos plumosa, in many respects, is similar to the Royal Palm. It has a smooth trunk, but is marked with rings. Its fronds are softer and more graceful (hence its name, plumosa.) It lacks, however, the smooth green leaf of the Royal; for near its own top the bases of old leaf stalks remain.

    The foliage of this Palm varies perhaps more than in any other, in the degree of its beauty. Some fronds will be thin and straggly while others are a lush green, almost sweeping the ground. This is due to the treatment it has received.

17

COCONUT
Cocos nucifera

The natural habitat of the Coconut Palm is not known but is believed to be in or near the Indian archipelago. It is now native to all tropical regions.

The coconut is perhaps the most important of all palms commercially. Practically all parts are useful.

The Coconut Palm flourishes when exposed to wind and water, thus it is adaptable to seaside planting.

Height 50 to 100 feet, usually with slender arched trunk and thick distended base.

Feathery leaves, or fronds 15 to 20 feet long, five feet long and two inches wide hanging from either side of a stiffly arched midrib form the graceful crown.

The bloom bracts with sprays of waxy, ivory-colored flowers and clusters of nuts are borne beneath the leaf crown. Older trees often can be observed bearing flowers, various-sized green nuts and the 12-to-15-inch-long, 10-inch-wide, light brown fibrous-husked mature nuts all at the same time. The roundish, hard-shelled monkey-faced nut is encased in the center of the husk.

Propagation is by seed only, and requiring several months for germination. The nut, still in the husk, is laid on its side with the broad, or stem end where the "eyes" are located and from which the sprout will emerge, slightly higher than bottom of the seed.

18

Coconut Palm

This Coconut Palm had clusters of large fruit when this picture was taken. It, like others planted in Central Florida, was killed in the freeze of 1958. More than 80 per cent of the Coconut trees were lost at that time. Although this Palm can be grown as far north as Tampa, it is definitely a tropical tree.

BOTTLE PALM

Mascarena lagenicaulis

This Palm is most attractive. The trunk is thick at
the bottom narrowing under the flowering area, thus
giving it its popular name. It is closely ringed and
rough; grows to about 15 feet. The fronds are a yellow-
ish-green and rather stiff, with a twist that makes them
distinctive. Its cousin the Spindle Palm (Mascarena
verschaffeltii) is also unusual. Growing taller, its trunk
is narrowed in the middle and swollen just under the
flowering area. Leaves of the Spindle are born in a
dense crown. Both Palms are easily identified. Flowers:
In double lines. Fruit: Black, rough and egg-shaped,
about one inch. Native habitat is the Mascarene Islands.

CANARY ISLAND DATE PALM — *Phoenix canariensis*

The Date Palm group (genus Phoenix) includes several species, most of which are found in Florida. The name "Phoenix" means purple, but it may also refer to the ancient country of Phoenicia. The Date Palm is one of the oldest of the cultivated plants and is referred to in ancient records.

Of this group, the Canary Island Date is one of the most beautiful. It can be safely planted in nearly all parts of Florida, being quite hardy and seldom injured by the cold. The tree has a spread of 30 feet and is easily recognized by its massive trunk often with hundreds of small ferns.

This palm is often called the Pineapple Palm because of its pineapple-shaped trunk.

Flowers are cream-white. The fruit is yellow and egg-shaped. This date is edible. The size is about three-quarters of an inch. They are found mostly in southern Florida, but, of course, are native to the Canary Islands.

CLIFF DATE PALM

Phoenix rupicola

This palm is very distinctive and easy to identify. Its rather slender trunk has bright green leaves that are soft and flat. They fairly glisten in the sun as they arch in a most attractive manner. It is unusual and especially adaptable to landscaping planting.

The flowers are cream-white; the fruit orange, about one-half inch in size. This Palm came originally from India, but now is a native of Florida.

The picture of this Cliff Date Palm taken in Clearwater, Florida, shows very plainly how the fronds arch from their base.

INDIA DATE PALM
Phoenix sylvestris

This is a tall, fast-growing Palm. It somewhat resembles the Phoenix canariensis, but with shorter leaves and a less massive trunk. It also attains a greater height.

A distinguishing characteristic of most specimens is the large mass of exposed roots at the base of the trunk. The tree is very symmetrical and quite attractive.

The blossoming period of many species of this genus occurs at the same time and has thus resulted in much inter-crossing. This has caused considerable confusion as to the correct identification.

The flowers are cream colored. The fruit is of an orange hue, and about one-half inch in size. They are native to India, but planted throughout Florida.

DATE PALM
Phoenix dactylifera

This Phoenix is the Common Date Palm of commerce. It is native to Egypt and Arabia but found in abundance in the United States. It often reaches a height of 90 to 100 feet with trunks roughly scarred. The Date Palm bears wherever it is found but only in arid climates such as California and Arizona is the fruit produced for commercial use.

Leaves, or fronds, 18 to 20 feet long, two to three feet wide, feathery, dark green with sharp spines at base near trunk.

Male and female flowers are borne in large clusters on separate trees. The fruit is an oblong berry with a grooved seed, a good tree usually bearing up to 200 pounds. The seeds also can be ground and used as a substitute for coffee.

Propagation is by seed, or by the suckers which develop at the base or on the side of the trunk which are removed when about five years old.

Commercial growing in this country was begun in the late 1800s, in Arizona, and was given added impetus with the importations of better varieties by W. T. Swingle of the U. S. Department of Agriculture.

Date Palm

This Date Palm in Clearwater has given as many as six pounds of fruit, proving that edible dates can be produced in Florida climate. These dates had excellent flavor, if not quite as much meat as those in arid climates.

SENEGAL DATE

Phoenix reclinata

A fast-growing tropical Palm native to Senegalese area in southeast Africa, found growing in thick clumps, 20 to 30 feet in height with rounded, matted crown of drooping fronds that often partially obscure five to a dozen or more reclining slender, shaggy trunks that have suckered from a common rootstock. When thinned out to five or six closely growing, tall, slender trunks, a pleasing effect is created. Constant pruning of suckers, however, is necessary to keep it from developing into a tangled mass as shown in the drawing above.

The bright green, stiffly curving feather-shaped leaf fronds are six to eight feet long with narrow, pointed leaflets 15 to 18 inches long.

Sprays of tiny cream-colored flowers are borne in the canoe-shaped spathes or buds produced on the clustered trunks. The sticky, ripening fruit, rusty-orange in color, about one inch long, is edible, but lacks the appetizing flavor of its close relative, the Phoenix dactylifera, the Date Palm of commerce. This is a rather important wine Palm in parts of Africa.

Although this Palm presents itself as a suitable landscape subject when the suckers are kept pruned, it seldom is used in closely planted areas because of the care needed to hold it in check. The Senegal Date will grow in North Florida, but constant care is necessary to protect it from frost.

Senegal Date Palm

This picture taken in Clearwater, Florida, shows the palm after the many suckers have been removed. It is about 25 to 30 years old.

The untrimmed Senegal Date forms a large and beautiful cluster. It often reaches the height of 25 feet and its long fronds practically touch the ground. Even in its beauty it is difficult to deal with because of its dangerous thorns.

PYGMY DATE PALM

Phoenix loueiri

Graceful Dwarf Palm, native of tropical Asia and Africa and widely grown in Florida as landscape subject and as potted house plant in northern states.

A true pygmy, it seldom exceeds ten feet in height with slender trunk five to six inches in diameter, covered with hard, protruding triangular basal ends of former leaf stems and presenting a geometrical pocked appearance at first glance.

Leaves, or fronds, three to four feet long, arched, with drooping, fringe-like dark-green leaflets, five to eight inches long, with sharp spines at base of leaf, near the trunk.

Canoe-shaped bloom spathes 12 to 14 inches long borne in lower leaf sheaths near crown. Small, greenish-yellow flowers on short spikes, in clusters, the male and female bloom produced on different plants. Seeds, about one-half inch long, oblong, with small, sharp spine at tip and seated acorn-like in tiny cup.

Discovered in Siam in the late nineteenth century by the German Roebelin.

Pigmy Date Palm

The Pigmy Date is ideal for interior decoration. It is dainty and attractive and its finely cut leaves are very graceful. It is used also in landscaping.

The Palm never grows very tall but is much more attractive when it is very short and its fronds almost touch the ground, as is shown in the picture.

ROYAL PALM

Roystonea regia

Royal Palms are among the handsomest of all Palms. Their smooth, cylindrical trunks look more like gray concrete pillars than living structures. These trunks are capped by a bright green super column of sheathing leaf bases which terminate in a beautiful crown of dark green feather-like leaves. Only the sheaf of the oldest leaf is visible in the 8 to 10-foot super column since it completely encircles and encloses the others.

The leaves, or fronds, are alternate, feathery, dark green from 12 to 25 feet long. They have numerous strap-like leaflets to three feet long at the base of leaf spine, decreasing in length to a few inches at tip producing a featherlike appearance.

Small fragrant, white flowers in thickly branched drooping clusters 18 inches to two feet long are borne at the leaf-sheath base (see illustration).

Fruits are dark red, almost purple about one-half inch in length—very abundant. Native to Cuba.

Roystonea elata—The Florida Royal Palm is very like the R. regia and often mistaken for it. The general characteristics are about the same. The fruit however, is more violet in color.

Royal Palms

The Royal Palm is well named and anyone who sees one is aware of its stately splendor. It is, however a tropical tree although it may be found up as far as Central Florida.

The clump shown in the picture is grown in a protected courtyard and has attained the height of 30 feet.

YELLOW BUTTERFLY PALM   *Chrysalidocarpus lutescens*

Also called Areca Palm; Cane Palm or Bamboo Palm.

Native to Madagascar.

Leaves, or fronds are pinnate, six to eight feet long with numerous dark leaflets 10 to 15 inches long, arching from a yellowish midriff.

Grows in clumps up to 40 feet in height with slender, yellow, smooth trunk, ringed, resembling the bamboo cane.

Short clusters of tiny, white, fragrant flowers are borne close to the crown. Oblong, three-quarters of an inch long, the fruit is yellowish-orange and turns a deep purple when mature.

Grown in South Florida as landscaping subject and as a pot plant everywhere for indoor ornamenting. Thrives best in a rich, fibrous soil.

An allied species, Areca cathecu, commonly called the Betel Nut Palm is definitely tropical. This single trunk variety produces an orange colored, nut-like seedfruit that is chewed by the Asiatic natives as a stimulant. It has a pungent flavor and the juice causes a black stain to be left on the teeth. The juice is also used as an astringent.

Yellow Butterfly Palm

This picture, taken in Clearwater, Florida, shows how decorative this Cluster Palm can be. It shows also the height to which it often grows.

This Palm thrives equally well in pots and is often used indoors where a green background is needed for decoration.

CHINESE FAN PALM   *Livistona chinensis*

The Chinese Fan Palm is the most common of the Livistona family, growing perhaps 30 feet and being well adapted to sub-tropical climates. The trunk is vaguely ringed and brownish.

The leaves are fan-shaped and have a definite lengthwise fold along the center. They are divided into some 50 or 60 long-pointed segments which droop gracefully at the ends.

The flowers are white and have an unpleasant odor. The fruit is dull metallic blue, olive shape, about one inch in diameter. Originally from China and Japan.

GRU-GRU PALM
Acroromia totai

The handsome Gru-Gru, or Acrocomia as it is sometimes called, often attains a height of 40 feet

The trunks are straight and cylindrical but armed with black spikes, making them unsuitable for general planting. The tree is topped with a mass of glossy green leaves. These are pinnate and resemble the Cocos plumosa, but are thicker and shorter.

Flowers are yellow and fruit is abundant. Originally from Argentina.

JELLY PALM
Butia capitata

The Jelly Palm belongs to a group of Palms formerly listed under the genus Cocos australis. They are easily identified because of their grayish green color and their pinnate leaves that curve and recurve. The trunk is covered with gray leaf bases, giving the plant a rugged appearance. A delicious clear jelly is often made from the fruit of this tree in its native habitat, South America.

In North America the tree is used only to give variety to ornamental planting. It is so hardy that it may be found in the northernmost part of the state and as far north as South Georgia.

The flower is yellow-lilac-reddish. The fruit, orange to yellow, egg-shaped and edible. Size about one inch. South America is their native habitat.

MANILA PALM   (*Adonidia merrillii*)   *Veitchia merrillii*

This Palm is one of the most beautiful growing in Florida. Some people call it the Little Royal, because of its crown of arching leaves which rise out of a bright upper column like the Royal Palm. It is a rapid grower from seed and once started to produce flowers and fruit, is scarcely without them. The brilliant red fruit seen in December gives it the name "The Christmas Palm."

The flowers are white; the fruit a brilliant red, and egg-shaped, hanging in showy clusters, about one and a half inch in size. Originally from the Philippines, this Palm is now quite common in South Florida.

37

KING PALM

Archontophoenix alexandrae

An Australian Palm native to Queensland and New South Wales and considered most graceful of all the Feather Palms. Often grows to height of 80 feet. Trunk usually seven to 12 inches thick at base, tapering to slightly bulging polished leaf sheaths underneath crown.

The King Palm has pinnate leaves 12 to 15 feet long with slender dark green leaflets that are glaucous white underneath. Leaf sheaths are milky oyster-white.

Flowers, white or creamy-white produced in large masses and followed by small bright red fruit. Seed, small, round with thin, fibrous covering.

The deep green feathery leaf-fronds are five to eight feet long with two-inch wide leaflets up to two and one-half feet long.

The King Palm is very like its cousin the Piccabeen Palm the Archontophoenix cunninghamiana. The flowers of the latter are lilac in color.

The King Palm requires a rich moist soil in a protected location. Young plants are very tender and very easily hurt by the cold, but will survive short periods of low temperature when mature.

This Palm is very stately and is much admired — and desired for planting.

Alexandria King Palm

This Palm is a graceful and rapid-growing tree. To the eye, they are quite beautiful, with smooth, slender trunks that sometimes reach 100 feet in height. These trunks are marked with scars which are left from fallen leaves.

The Alexandria King is of this family. It is topped with a crown of narrow pinnate leaves that have very regular segments. They are green on top and rather shiny white underneath. The secondary rib or nerves are very prominent. The trunk is somewhat enlarged toward the base.

FLORIDA THATCH PALM

Thrinax parviflora

Thatch Palms are found generally on the southern tip of Florida. All have slender, graceful trunks rising 25 or 35 feet. The fan-shaped leaves make almost a complete circle and are often utilized as a covering for shelters.

The Florida Thatch Palm has a slender trunk about six inches in diameter. The green leaves have wide segments that are cleft halfway or more the length of the leaf, and are a shining yellowish color.

The flowers grow close together and the fruit is white, globular, about one-fourth inch in size.

FLORIDA SILVER PALM   *Cocothrinax argentata*

This delightful little Palm is definitely of the southern climate. The above picture taken at Fairchild Gardens, Coconut Grove, near Miami shows its characteristics. It is very slender, not exceeding six inches in diameter. It is smooth and rather slate colored.

Its fan-shaped leaves are almost circular and fairly thin. They are glossy green on the top and silvery underneath. When the wind tosses their leaves it is easy to see how they came by the name of "Silver Palm".

The Palm can attain a height of 20 feet, although the majority of trees are not more than three feet tall. They sometimes branch at the base to form a cluster.

The fruit is about one-half inch in diameter and the meat very dark, almost black. The Silver Palm is native to Florida.

FISH TAIL PALM
Caryota ureus

Also called Wine Palm, Toddy Palm and **Jaggery** Palm.

Native to Asia and Australia. Often reaches height of 60 feet, with ringed, brown trunks one to one and one-half feet diameter, smooth after leaf sheaths have fallen.

Leaves are dark green, to 20 feet long and 10 to 15 feet wide, the leaflets stiff and prominently notched with wedge-shaped divisions that somewhat resemble a fish's tail from which the common name is derived.

Flowers borne in axils of leaves in large clusters of plume-like racemes which very often is likened to a horse's tail. Although the trees do not bloom until maturity and die after fruiting, the process may require several years as all of the species start flowering from the topmost leaf axil downward until the very bottom one has produced a bloom. Seeds are reddish-black, round or kidney-shaped.

Similar to the above is the Caryota mitis, which suckers freely and generally is seen growing in clumps of six or more smooth stems.

The fruit of the Fish Tail Palm is not only inedible, it is dangerous to eat.

Fish Tail Palms

This Fish Tail Palm is a rather fast grower and needs extra space. It is a lovely tree, as this picture shows. It is seen here, however growing in a narrow parkway. It was later transferred to a lawn where because of its size it was much more impressive.

MacARTHUR PALM
Actinophloeus macarthuri

This is a cluster palm, an attractive, slender, grey-trunk species that grows at times to 25 feet. The pinnate leaves are a bright dark-green. The individual leaflets are obliquely cut at the ends as if they have been bitten off.

The flowers are white. The fruit is green at first, then turns red, about one-half inch in diameter.

They are originally from New Guinea.

BROAD LEAF LADY PALM
Rhapis excelsa

The Raphis is a family of slender reed-like Palms that form dense clusters. The numerous trunks may reach a height of 15 feet. They will be about two inches in diameter and smooth green, prominently ringed, usually covered with fibrous material.

The palmate leaves are about two and a half feet across, glossy green and deeply cut into many segments which are slightly drooping with the ends blunt although toothed.

Flowers are yellowish in color. The fruit is brownish-purple, pear-shaped, about one-half inch in size.

They are native to South China and Japan.

This variety is good where mass foliage is wanted. Well adapted to partial shade.

AFRICAN OIL PALM
Elaeis guineensis

A native tropical African palm with long, arched, feathery, 15-feet-long leaves or fronds very similar to the Date Palm. The trunk, immediately below the leaves, is covered with a fibrous matting much like that of the Coconut Palm and often attains a height of 50 or more feet.

Flowers are borne when the Palm is but three or four years old. The red or yellow nut-like fruit, about the size of a hickory nut, is produced in large, closely compacted clusters with sharp, protruding spines. Pulp of fruit is edible as is the seed.

Cultivated commercially in its native Africa and the East Indies for "palm ofl" used in soap and ointments.

Although rare in this country, it could well be adapted to South Florida as a beautiful ornamental and very likely could be cultivated in sufficient quantities to make it a commercial attribute to the State. Growing conditions are very much the same for this Palm as for other tropical species introduced into the State.

Although Palms generally are associated with high temperatures, many actually suffer more from exposure to the intense direct heat of the sun than from cold.

46

African Oil Palm

There are not very many African Oil Palms in Florida but it is a very ornamental tree. The one pictured above is at the Fairchild Tropical Gardens in Miami. With its graceful leaves which are dark green and its massive trunk which is covered with fibre, it makes a most unusual picture.

You will note from the size of the tree that a great deal of space should be set aside for its growth. On anything short of an estate this African Oil Palm would definitely be crowded.

Because this Palm has become well adapted to Southern Florida, there is some conjecture as to whether or not it might be grown for commercial use. At present its virtue is confined to ornamentation. In that field it excels.

SUGAR PALM
Arenga saccharifera

This is a massive Palm under cultivation because of its height and tremendous fronds. The leaves are a very dark green and sweep upwards. They are sometimes 28 feet long and six feet wide.

The trunks while young are covered with old leaf stalks and coarse black fibers. This gives it a dark, unkempt appearance. Native of India.

This Palm where native is one of the chief sources of sugar, which is obtained by cutting the flower clusters. The fiber also is valuable for cord.

The flowers, male, green with violet petals; female. all green. The fruit is yellow and purple-yellow, globular in shape and about two inches in diameter.

SOLITAIRE PALM   *Ptychosperma elegans* (*Seforthia elegans*)

The Solitaire Palm is a beautiful small tree that is well adapted to small lawns or group plantings. The ringed trunk which is somewhat enlarged at the base is about four inches thick. The leaves are erect and arching, having 20 or more pairs of fairly wide pinnate leaves. The clasping leaf sheaths make a small upper shaft or column.

The name Seforthia or Alexandra is sometimes used to designate this Palm. Flowers: White. Fruit. Red, almost round; ¼ inch. Native Australia.

PRINCESS PALM
Dictyosperma album

The Princess Palm, sometimes called the Hurricane Palm is very tall and stately. Its dark grey trunk with rings at its base, is about 8 inches in diameter and rises to about 35 feet. The leaves are graceful and spreading, with the individual leaflets slightly drooping. These leaves are often 12 feet long with the individual leaflets reaching two feet and two inches wide. Ends are split.

Flowers reddish-yellow, fragrant. Fruit, egg-shaped purplish, about half inch. Habitat Mascerne Islands.

SAGO PALM
Cycas revoluta

Although the Sago resembles a Palm it is not one. Instead it is a Cycad (Cycas), which is the oldest known species of seed bearing plants.

It is a slow-growing plant native to Japan. The Sago may reach a height of 10 feet but it is most often seen much smaller. It has a palm-like trunk about a foot in diameter which is surrounded with stiff shiny dark green leaves. These leaves are arranged in the form of a rosette. They are from three to five feet long with leaflets extending from the main midrib about four or five inches.

As with all Cycads, the male and female flowers are produced on different plants. The cones which hold these flowers both grow at the top of the trunk but the male cone is elongated while the female cone is round and dome-like. Both are yellowish-orange and showy. The seeds are born in a cluster of what looks like dwarf leaves around the female cone. These, as well as the larger leaves of the Sago are very desirable for flower arrangements.

They are in demand for the making of funeral designs and are also sought in the decorating of churches for Palm Sunday.

These plants are tropical in appearance and add distinction to a garden.

FERN PALM
Cycas circinalis

The Fern Palm, like the Sago Palm, is one of the family of Cycads, which closely resemble true Palms. Resemblance is closer to the Sago Palm in that it has rich, dark green pinnate leaves growing from a pithy stem, but the leaves of the Fern Palm are usually much longer and have a softer, more feathery, fern-like appearance.

Like all cycads the Fern Palm bears male and female flowers on separate plants. The male flowers are produced in an elongated cone that as it matures gives off a rather objectionable odor. The female cone is round and less conspicious. It is often sought, however, for flower arrangements.

This plant grows rapidly and very luxuriantly. Along the stem there are often found many suckers which, if they are removed may be started as new plants. These cycads, because of their very dark green foliage, add much to a landscape. They are used a great deal in ornamental plantings. The leaves are also valuable for decorating.

COONTIE (SEMINOLE BREAD)   *Zamia integrifolia*

Of the family Cycads, the Zamias are closely allied to the Palms and should be included in the study of fibrous trees. The Coontie, which grows wild, is one of the most primitive of seed-bearing plants. They are a staple with the Seminoles in South Florida and much folklore is wrapped around their usefulness.

The Coontie is a fern-like plant with rather stiff leaves. The plant tends to be circular with the fruit in the center. Like the other Cycads, they are either male or female. The fruits of the latter are much more showy —reddish-brown pods that open to show scarlet seeds. The male fruit is long and thin. The leaves of the Coontie as well as the fruit pods are used extensively in flower arrangements.

The large underground stems contain a starch-like substance that the Seminole Indians have utilized for a kind of bread. This has given the Coontie its nickname "Seminole Bread." There is, however, present in this substance a certain amount of poison. The Indians have learned to remove this by frequent washings and kneadings. The commercial name of Arrowroot has been given to this product. It is interesting to note that the Zamias in some other parts of the world have a poison that is not so mild. It is so potent in fact that it has been used in assassinations. The plant can be brought under cultivation and it thrives, but grows very slowly.

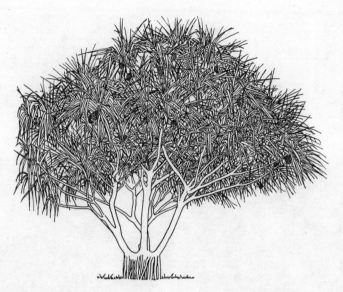

PANDANUS

Pandanus veitchii

Also called Screw Pine.
Member Screw Pine Family (Pandanaceae).

Tropical Old World plant growing 30 to 40 feet high with slender trunks, palm-like, and usually supported by immense prop roots that appear to be lifting the tree from the soil.

The common name—Screw Pine—is derived from the spiral growth-habit of the prickly-margined swordlike leaves. These leaves are narrow (about 3 inches) and grow several feet long.

Flowers are small and borne in close spikes or heads.

The fruit of the Screw Pine is a mass of woody nuts that hang picturesquely in a large ball, and are edible. Like other tropical plants the tree is useful. The roots are often used for the making of ropes and baskets. The leaves are woven into mats and hats. The leaves are also collected for the making of paper.

Much hardier than the Palms, it is grown throughout South Florida and occasionally in protected areas in Central area of the state.

Propagation is by seeds or by suckers growing from stem base of plant. When suckers are taken for growing-on into individual plants, remove when very small. This is done with point of knife blade. Pot singly in small container using a sandy-loam mixture and water sparingly until roots are formed. Young potted specimens make excellent house or patio plants.

54

Screw Pine

This Screw Pine is an attractive addition to the garden of the Wedgwood Inn of St. Petersburg, Florida.
When in fruit it has many clusters of nuts that give it
a tropical appearance. With roots above ground the
tree seems to walk on stilts.

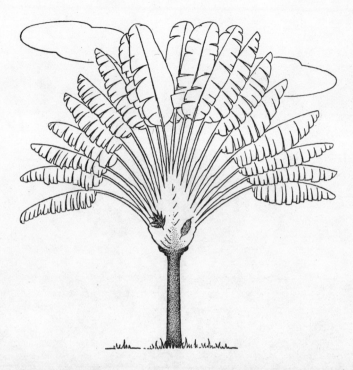

TRAVELERS TREE   *Ravenala madagascariensis*

Member Banana Family (Musaceae)

A remarkable tropical plant with palm-like trunk up to one foot or more in diameter sometimes reaching height of 30 feet with broad fan-shaped top of long banana-like leaves.

Leaves range up to 10 feet long, 12 to 20 inches wide with heavy arching midrib, older leaves having many splits in side sections.

Small white flowers are borne in canoe-like pods or bracts all attached to a single erect stalk. Seeds are black with bluish shell or husk which drops away as seeds ripen.

Like the banana, water is stored in the bases of the leaf stalks which naturally would be a welcome find for the weary, thirsty traveler.

The large leaves grow very symetrically, often attaining a length of 15 feet. They are easily frayed by the winds but this seemingly has little effect on the ornamental value of the tree. This species differs so materially from the other trees in shape and appearance that it is often included in a garden when an uncommon plant is wanted. Native to Madagascar,

Travelers Tree

This picture taken in Clearwater, Florida is of a very young tree. The leaves even in this specimen have begun to be frayed by the wind. The blossoms and fruit will come later at the base of the stalks. This tree if allowed to sucker will form an attractive clump for the garden. Note the heavy stalks that are quite hollow and store liquid.

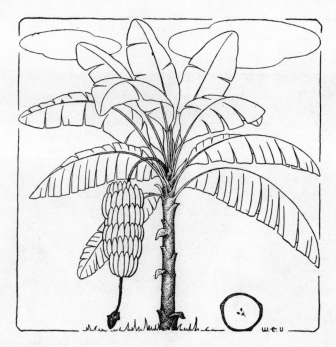

BANANA

Musaceae

Very large herb-like perennial native to tropical Asia and grown throughout the tropical and subtropical world. In favorable conditions it usually attains height of nine to 20 feet in from 10 to 15 months after planting. Often grown as ornamentals and sometimes produce fruit in milder areas of California, Louisiana and the seaboard sections of the Gulf States. Banana culture in the United States, however, is largely confined to Florida south of Fort Pierce and Tampa.

The thick, soft stalk or false trunk is composed of accumulated layers of the bases of leaf sheaths, with crown of bright green leaves, four to nine feet long and up to two feet wide, depending upon variety. The tender leaves usually are torn to shreds by strong winds unless planted in a sheltered location. Short periods of cold will not kill the plant, but it does destroy any chance of obtaining fruit.

When the plant reaches flowering age, the huge purplish bud emerges from the center of the crown. In a few days the floral stalk has grown long enough to extend downward, and the leathery bracts or flower sheaths with reddish inner lining, open successively as the bud stalk develops, exposing tiered rows of yellowish-white tube-like flowers.

58

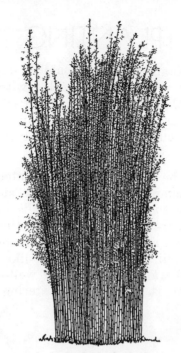

BAMBOO   *Bambusae*

A tropical hollow-stem perennial including several species, natives of the warmer parts of Asia, Africa, and South America and widely distributed in the tropical and subtropical regions of both continents. The most important is Banbusa arundinaceae, growing to 70 feet or more, the stems attaining a diameter of five or six inches and are used for building, furniture-making and many other utilitarian purposes. Several smaller species including Bambusa multiplex, Phyllostachys aurea and Bambusa vulgaris, all of which range in height from 30 to 40 feet, and Bambusa nana, seldom over 10 feet, are much used as garden subjects for special effects. The latter, B. nana, has bluish-green leaves which often are marked with splotches of yellow, pinkish-red and silver.

Inconspicuous flowers are borne in many species, especially B. arundinaceae which dies after flowering. Because of the unreliability of flowering it is difficult to obtain seed and propagation almost wholly is by layering or division of root clumps.

Bamboos require partial shade and should be planted in deep, rich loam and watered frequently when rainfall is insufficient to keep the ground moist, especially during the spring and summer growing seasons.

PLANTING

Holes for planting Palms should be dug much larger than the size of the plant and filled with compost, decayed leaves and grass cuttings, well rotted manure, muck and clay if soil is too sandy. The addition of bone meal is good. This should be prepared two months in advance if possible.

Palms may be planted or transplanted at any time, but the rainy summer months are best, since that is the time of vigorous root growth and also the time when nature produces more water. In transplanting, trees should be put in at least as deep as they were before. Fill the hole with top soil, making a saucer-like depression to collect and hold water. A mulch of well-rotted manure, peat, or leaves is advisable. Watering must not be neglected.

PRUNING

The pruning of Palms usually means the trimming off of leaves and floral parts as they turn brown and become unsightly. Palms make their growth from center leaves and these should not be disturbed. In pruning clustering Palms the stems that are too tall may be cut out rather than back. This will allow others to grow up to take their place. Severe pruning of outer leaves is necessary when Palms are transplanted. The palm-leafed variety require even closer pruning than the feather-leafed variety.

The University of Florida is continually making experiments and giving out additional information. Every Floridian should know of this service and appreciate it. The address has been given in the front of this book.

PROPAGATION

Palms are grown from seeds, off - shoots or from the division of clusters. A few trees like the true Date puts out shoots near its base and these may be removed when young in order to start new ones. Some of the clustering Palms, where several stems are present, may be safely divided when the plant is young. This is true of the Yellow Butterfly.

With the majority of Palms, seeds are the sole method of obtaining new plants. Seeds should be planted as soon as possible after maturity. They need to be covered with soil from 1/8 to 1 inch and kept moist during the time of germination. Some seeds such as those of the Phoenix or Washingtonia will require only three or four weeks. Others like the Butia will take from two to four months. There are known instances of seeds sprouting after three years.

Whatever container is used for the seeds should have holes or cracks in the bottom for drainage. The soil should be kept moist but not wet. Complete drying out should be avoided because intermittent soaking and drying prevents germination. On the other hand too much moisture causes "damping off."

Seedlings may be potted when an inch or so high. It is advisable to do so before too much rootage has formed. Potting soil that will give good results can be made of a mixture of sod and manure that is well decayed.

In planting Coconuts, the nuts are placed on their sides and buried only about 1/2 of their thickness, leaving the upper half fully exposed. Again the ground must be kept moist. Germination requires from one to five months. The Coconut may be transplanted when the leaf reaches a height of about one foot, even if there are few or no roots showing.

FERTILIZING

Palms like organic fertilizer. Cottonseed meal, ground steamed bone meal, tankage, blood, guano, fish scraps and manures are good. These are best planted with the new Palm but may be used in combination in early spring. From 10 to 25 pounds of such fertilizer may be used—being scattered under the leaf spread.

Commercial fertilizers in the proportion of 4-6-8 also meet the requirement of Palms. This may be used in quantities of from two ounces for very small plants to 15 pounds for large trees. In northern Florida, two applications per year should be given, one in late winter or early spring and the other in mid-summer. Further south, where growing is continuous, a third application in late summer or early fall is advisable.

Fertilizer may be applied broadcast under the leaf spread, but if Palms are planted in lawns, "plugging" is advisable. This is done by making holes (with a crowbar or like instrument). The holes should be about one foot deep and two feet apart some distance from the trunk of the tree. These are filled with fertilizer and then closed.

Some Palms, such as the Cocos plumosa, suffer from a frizzly condition which is identified as a manganese deficiency. The first symptom to appear is the lack of color in the leaves. This is followed by a frizzling and final death of the leaf. One treatment a year of manganese sulphate is usually sufficient to restore the tree. The dose suggested is one half to six pounds of 65 per cent manganese sulfate per plant, depending on size of the plant.

Other Palms showing symptoms similar to the Cocos are: Royals Gru-Gru, Fish Tail and Chinese Fan Palms. The similarity of symptoms suggests manganese treatment on other species.

INDEX